What Is a Thunderstorm?

Robin Johnson

 Crabtree Publishing Company

www.crabtreebooks.com

Author: Robin Johnson

Publishing plan research and development: Reagan Miller

Editors: Reagan Miller and Kathy Middleton

Proofreaders: Janine Deschenes

Design and photo research: Samara Parent

Prepress technician: Samara Parent

Print and production coordinator: Kathy Berti

Photographs
iStock: p9 (top right)
Shutterstock: p18 © Glynnis Jones

All other images from Shutterstock

About the author
Robin Johnson has written more than 60 educational books for children. She plans to keep writing books and chasing rainbows—whatever the weather.

Library and Archives Canada Cataloguing in Publication

Johnson, Robin (Robin R.), author
    What is a thunderstorm? / Robin Johnson.

(Severe weather close-up)
Includes index.
Issued in print and electronic formats.
ISBN 978-0-7787-2400-1 (bound).--ISBN 978-0-7787-2437-7
(paperback).-- ISBN 978-1-4271-1752-6 (html)

    1. Thunderstorms--Juvenile literature. I. Title.

QC968.2.J65 2016   j551.55'4   C2015-908684-1
                                         C2015-908685-X

Library of Congress Cataloging-in-Publication Data

CIP available at the Library of Congress

Crabtree Publishing Company

Printed in Canada/032016/EF20160210

www.crabtreebooks.com   1-800-387-7650

Published in Canada
Crabtree Publishing
616 Welland Ave.
St. Catharines, Ontario
L2M 5V6

Published in the United States
Crabtree Publishing
PMB 59051
350 Fifth Avenue, 59th Floor
New York, New York 10118

Published in the United Kingdom
Crabtree Publishing
Maritime House
Basin Road North, Hove
BN41 1WR

Published in Australia
Crabtree Publishing
3 Charles Street
Coburg North
VIC 3058

Contents

Cloud spotting

Have you ever stared up at the clouds? Sometimes they look like shapes. You can spot sheep or other animals in them. You can see silly faces. Clouds can be fun to watch. But some clouds can bring bad **weather**.

What does the shape of this fluffy cloud remind you of?

What is weather?

Weather is what the air and sky are like in a certain place at a certain time. Clouds, sunlight, **wind**, and **precipitation** are all parts of weather. Wind is moving air. Precipitation is rain, snow, or other water that falls from the clouds.

Stormy weather

On some days, the weather is pleasant. On other days, it is not. Periods of bad weather are called storms. Some storms have strong winds. Others bring a lot of rain, snow, or other precipitation.

Winter is cold and snowy. Storms bring a heavy fall of snow.

The weather is warm and rainy in spring.

Storm seasons

What do you Think?

Why do different types of storms happen in different seasons?

Different kinds of storms happen during different **seasons**. A season is a time of year with certain weather. The seasons are winter, spring, summer, and fall. In spring and summer, many places get strong storms called **thunderstorms**.

Summer is hot and sunny.

The weather is cool and windy in fall.

7

What are thunderstorms?

The sky is filled with dark, gray clouds. Suddenly, a flash of **lightning** shoots from a cloud. Next, you hear the sound of **thunder**. Large raindrops beat fast and hard against the window. What is happening?

It is a thunderstorm!

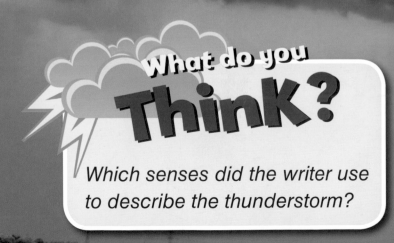

What do you ThinK?

Which senses did the writer use to describe the thunderstorm?

Signs of a storm

A thunderstorm has strong winds, heavy rain, thunder, and lightning. Thunder is a deep rumbling sound or loud crashing noise. It is the sound lightning makes when it moves through air. Thunderstorms sometimes have **hail**. Hail is small balls of ice that fall from the clouds.

hail

Lightning is a bright flash of light in the sky.

Severe weather

Thunderstorms are a type of **severe weather**. Weather that is severe, or very strong, can damage buildings and land. It can also be harmful to people and animals. Thunderstorms are dangerous because of lightning, which can strike anywhere without warning.

Thunderstorms can be scary, but they usually end in less than 30 minutes.

Lightning strikes

Lightning is flow of **electricity** that looks like a streak of light in the sky. Lightning often hits tall objects, such as trees and mountains. But it can also hit anything else on the ground. When lightning strikes, objects can break or catch fire. People and animals can be badly burned or killed.

Thunderstorms are also called electrical storms.

What do you ThinK?

Why do adults warn you not to stand under a tree for shelter during a thunderstorm?

How thunderstorms form

Thunderstorms begin when the Sun heats **moist** air near the ground. The warm air rises quickly and cools. It cools because the **temperature** up in the sky is lower than it is near the ground. Tiny drops of water form in the cold air. The water drops come together and make clouds that grow very tall and are flat on top.

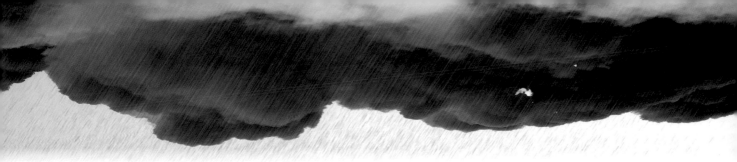

Electricity in the air

Thunderstorm clouds grow high into the air, where the temperature is even cooler. Freezing temperatures turn some water drops into bits of ice. Moving air causes the ice and water to bump into each other. Each time they bump together, they make electricity. Electricity builds up in the clouds until it is released as lightning.

We usually hear thunder after we see lightning. It can be very loud!

Safe places

If you are outside and you see gray clouds or hear thunder, hurry to a safe place before the storm begins. Go inside your house, school, or other nearby building. Another safe place to stay is inside a car or truck. If there are no buildings or cars nearby, crouch down on the balls of your feet away from tall trees. Do not lie down. Lightning can travel along the ground, so the less your body touches the ground the safer you are!

Rubber tires help keep a car safe from any electricity on the ground. Roll up the windows and do not touch any parts made of metal.

Unsafe spaces

Metal and water are **conductors** of electricity. That means electricity passes through them easily—right to you! You should never hide from thunderstorms under bleachers, near fences, inside sheds or tents, or in any other place that is made of metal or has metal parts. Also, do not go swimming or ride in boats during thunderstorms.

Remember to bring your pets indoors, too! Metal chains and doghouses are not safe for dogs during thunderstorms.

What do you ThinK?

An umbrella keeps you dry when it rains. But why should you never use one during a thunderstorm?

Indoor safety

You should be safe from thunderstorms when you are indoors. But you must be careful there as well. Stay away from windows and doors. Lightning could travel through cracks or spaces in them. Strong winds, heavy rain, or blowing objects could also break the glass.

When thunder roars, go indoors!

Unplug and stay dry

During thunderstorms, do not use televisions, computers, or other objects that use electricity. Do not take baths or wash your hands. Water pipes and electrical wires are conductors. They can carry lightning from other places into your home.

During a thunderstorm, you might get a shock if you touch a water tap or an object that uses electricity.

After the storm

After a thunderstorm passes, do not leave your safe place right away. Wait at least 30 minutes after the last sound of thunder before you go outdoors. Even though the sky may be clear and sunny, lightning could still strike! It can travel long distances from storm clouds.

*Strong winds and falling trees can knock over **power lines**. Stay away from the power lines and anything they touch.*

*When a lot of rain falls in a short period of time, **floods** can happen.*

ROAD SUBJECT TO
FLOODING
INDICATORS SHOW DEPTH

Watch for damage

There may be damage after a thunderstorm. Watch for fallen tree branches, broken glass, and other dangers. If a power line is down, do not touch it. Electricity may still be flowing through it. Stay away from ponds, creeks, or rivers. They are dangerous places after a heavy rain!

Weather warnings

Meteorologists warn us when thunderstorms are coming to our area. Meteorologists are scientists who study weather. They measure wind, rain, and other parts of weather to **predict** thunderstorms. They report severe weather so people can prepare and stay safe. You can find weather reports on television, on the radio, or online.

Clouds that look like thin, white sheets covering the sky tell you that wet weather is coming later that day or the next day.

Thin, white clouds that stretch high across the sky mean the weather will be nice for a while, but it will change by the next day.

Head in the clouds

Now it is your turn to be a meteorologist! Study the sky in the afternoon or evening during the spring or summer. That is when most thunderstorms take place. If there are clouds in the sky, draw them in a notebook. Use the pictures on these pages to help you identify them.

Low, dark, gray clouds are filled with water. If it is not raining now, it will be soon!

Some clouds look like cotton balls! These low, fluffy, white clouds mean the weather will be nice.

Tall, fluffy, white clouds that have flat, wide tops bring thunderstorms.

Patterns that predict

After you have drawn your clouds, watch what the weather is like later the same day. Is it dry or rainy? Is there a thunderstorm? Write down what the clouds and weather are like for several days. Soon you will see a **pattern**. You will learn which type of cloud brings thunderstorms. Then you can predict when a thunderstorm will strike!

What do you Think?

Why is it important to know when thunderstorms will happen?

Learning more

Books

Changing Weather: Storms by Kelley MacAulay and Bobbie Kalman. Crabtree Publishing Company, 2006.

The Water Cycle by Bobbie Kalman and Rebecca Sjonger. Crabtree Publishing Company, 2006.

Thunder and Lightning by Helen Cox Cannons. Heinemann, 2014.

Websites

Be a weather whiz kid and learn all about thunderstorms at:
www.weatherwizkids.com/weather-thunderstorms.htm

Find storm stories, activities, quizzes, maps, and more at:
www.eo.ucar.edu/kids/dangerwx/tstorm1.htm

Learn how to keep safe—and calm—when thunderstorms strike:
http://kidshealth.org/kid/watch/out/thunderstorms.html

Do a puzzle and learn all about clouds at NASA's website:
http://spaceplace.nasa.gov/cloud-scramble/en/

Words to know

Note: Some boldfaced words are defined where they appear in the book.

conductors (kuhn-DUHK-ters) noun Things that electricity passes through easily

electricity (ih-lek-TRIS-i-tee) noun A form of energy found in nature that can also be made by people

floods (fluhds) noun Water flowing onto areas that are usually dry

lightning (LAHYT-ning) noun A bolt of electricity that is released from clouds

moist (moist) adjective Describing something that is slightly wet

pattern (PAT-ern) noun Something that repeats

power lines (POU-er lahyn) noun A metal line, or cable, that is used to carry electricity from one place to another

predict (pri-DIKT) verb To tell what will happen before it takes place

severe weather (suh-VEER WETH-er) adjective, noun Dangerous weather that can cause damage and hurt people and animals

temperature (TEHM-per-a-chur) noun How cold or warm the air is

thunder (THUHN-der) noun The sound lightning makes when it travels through air

thunderstorms (THUHN-der-stawrms) noun Storms that have lightning and thunder

A noun is a person, place, or thing. A verb is an action word that tells you what someone or something does. An adjective is a word that tells you what something is like.

Index